IMPOSSIBLE CREATURES:
A Bestiary

By Katherine Mosby

Drawings by Jennifer Wulfe

Introduction

This alphabet book borrows from the tradition of the medieval bestiary in its attempt to catalogue the monsters of the day. All of the imaginary creatures, identified with a rhymed couplet, are more than familiar to us in their foibles and will resonate to anyone who has been an exasperated host, embarrassed friend, irritated spouse, or self-examining soul.

Since these social monsters are also inescapable and sometimes even irresistible, they will find themselves at home in every library. They are whimsical versions of who we are when we misbehave: the social animal running amok in the drawing room or conference room or dinner table. The chivalric task we now face is no longer to slay the beast but to tame it, or at least to name it.

A is for the Anagoth
    who is fitful and snippy and given
to sloth.

B is for the Boragoon
who sings all the time
but never in tune.

C is for the Carnatine

a rage of loud colors

in permanent preen.

D is for the Dormophile
who, when awoken,
is perfectly vile.

E is for the Emphatant
    who has two modes: the
rave and the rant.

F is for the Furry Slur.
   Salacious gossip makes it
purrrr...

G is for the famous Gavort who'll finish the chocolate, cherries, and port.

H is for the Hedonate
who has six vices—
no, make that eight.

I is for the Icantop,
a collection of names
waiting to drop.

J is for the Jabolite
so anxious to please,
he's over-polite.

K is for the Kommisaurus
whose touted ideals
are oddly porous.

L is for the Lugubrum.
Conversation is dull
when it isn't dumb.

M is for the Megastint,
a compulsive collector
who saves even lint.

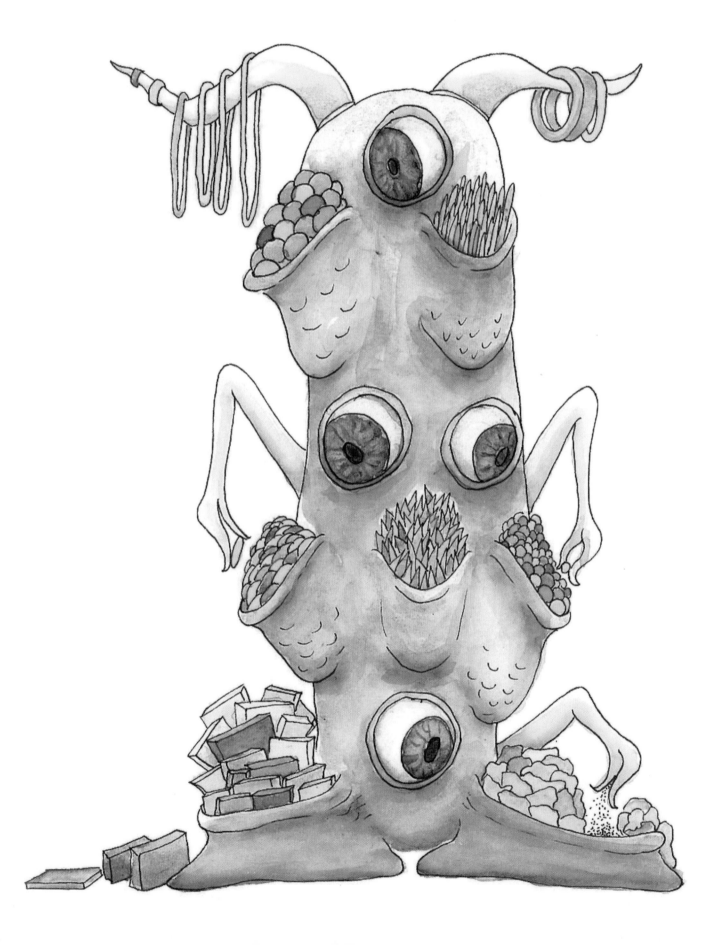

N is for the Neonorious
whose righteous intolerance
is neigh notorious.

O is for the Ohlalator
full of surprises we've all
seen before.

P is for the Predatorus
whom we didn't invite
because he would gore us.

Q is for the Quivering Quelp
who puts such stock
in Freudian help.

R is for the Rhetorix.
Compulsive puns
are one of its tics.

S is for the Slagoress
with a curious knack
for making a mess.

T is for the Tetramundo
a terrible pendant,
waxing profundo.

U is for the Uttermutter.
The suggestion of work
sets its heart aflutter.

V is for the Vanogryph
who reeks of ego.
    just take a whiff.

W is for the Walalinx,
so unabashed
        after just a few drinks.

X is for the Xereth
whose every breath
reminds us of death.

Y is for the Yammerbeak
who speaks at great length
in Latin and Greek.

Libellus

Z is for the fatalist Zed
who will tell you it's safer
to just stay in bed.

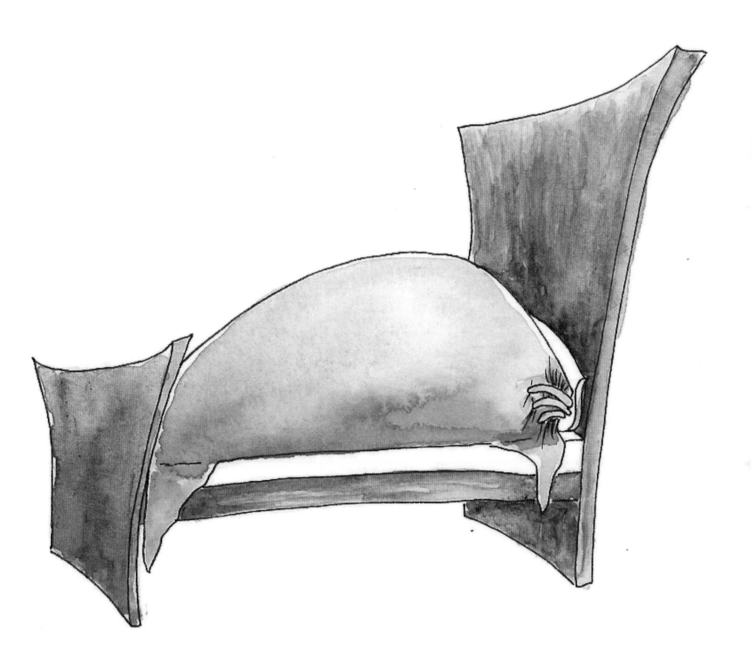

The End.